P A C E M A [

# American Government

# WORKBOOK

Upper Saddle River, New Jersey
www.globefearon.com

# Pacemaker® American Government Third Edition

## Reviewers

We thank the following educators, who provided valuable comments and suggestions during the development of this book:

**Pacemaker Curriculum Advisor:** Stephen C. Larsen, formerly of the University of Texas at Austin
**Subject Area Consultant:** Gerri Cassinelli, Rolling Hills Middle School,
Cupertino, California

*Executive Editor:* Jane Petlinski
*Project Manager:* Suzanne Keezer
*Project Editor:* Renée Beach
*Associate Production Editor:* Amy Benefiel
*Lead Designer:* Joan Jacobus
*Market Manager:* Katie Erezuma
*Manufacturing Supervisor:* Mark Cirillo
*Series Cover Design:* Evelyn Bauer

## About the Cover

The Constitution created three branches of government. The executive branch is led by the President and Vice President. The legislative branch is made up of Congress. The judicial branch is made up of the courts. What images from the cover relate to each branch of government?

ISBN: 0-130-23618-7

Printed in the United States of America

2 3 4 5 6 7 8 9 10          04 03 02 01

1-800-848-9500
www.globefearon.com

# Contents

# A Note to the Student

The exercises in this workbook go along with your *Pacemaker American Government* textbook. Each exercise in this workbook is linked to a chapter in your textbook. This workbook gives you the opportunity to do three things—review, practice, and think critically.

The review exercises are questions and activities that test your knowledge of the information presented in the textbook. Set goals for yourself and try to meet them as you complete each activity. Being able to remember and apply information is an important skill, and leads to success on tests, in school, at work, and in life.

The skill practice exercises help you to apply government and social studies skills. You will need these skills as you read and write about the information you have learned in your textbook. Some pages in the workbook have charts and graphic organizers. These pages will give you extra practice in using your chart skills and in working with graphic organizers.

Your critical thinking skills are challenged when you complete the critical thinking exercises. Critical thinking— or to put it another way, thinking critically—means putting information to use. For example, you may review and recall information about how the Constitution was written. Later, you might use that information to explain why and how your rights as a citizen are protected. When you apply what you know to a different situation, you are thinking critically.

Your textbook is a wonderful source of knowledge. By using it along with this workbook, you will learn a great deal about government. The real value of the information will come when you have mastered the skills and put them to use by thinking critically.

Name _____ Date _____

 **1 ▸ Defining Point of View**                          **Exercise 1**

*Critical Thinking*

A point of view is a certain way of looking at things. A person's beliefs,
attitudes, and opinions largely depend on that person's point of view. Point of
view is determined by one's past experiences. Read the two different points
of view below. Think about these terms as you read:

| dictator | laws | republic | voting | elect | choice |
|----------|------|----------|--------|-------|--------|

**A.** Fredrik says this about his country.

My country has a new president. Our president was once head of the army. But
our country is in trouble. People need jobs. There isn't enough food for everyone.
So the army general made himself president. Now he makes the laws for everyone.
In my country, no one votes. I don't think people need to vote. Our president
knows how to run things. He knows better than the people. Soon, life in my
country will be better. We don't have to worry. The president will take care of us.

**B.** Felicia says this about her country.

My country is very large. I think it is too large for everyone to make the laws.
Instead, we elect representatives. The elected representatives make the laws. What
can we do if we don't like the laws? We ask our representatives to change them.
But what if our representatives don't do what most people want? Then we vote for
someone else in the next election. I like the way my country works. People really
have a say in their government.

**Answer the questions below in complete sentences. Use the terms above to
help you.**

**1.** What kind of government does Fredrik's country have?

_____

**2.** What does Fredrik like about his government?

_____

**3.** What kind of government does Felicia's country have?

_____

**4.** Why does Felicia like the way her country works?

_____

**5.** Which country described above gives people more choices?

_____

## 1 ▸ Defining Words                    Exercise 2

**Read the passage below. Then, in your own words, write definitions for the underlined words.**

> Frederick Douglass High School has its own <u>constitution</u>. It contains <u>laws</u> for the school's 2,000 students. The rules are for all students, but not all the students wrote the rules. The rules were written by 15 student <u>representatives</u>. Who picked the representatives? All of the students did. They voted for the representatives in an <u>election</u>. The representatives form the school's government. Some of the rules or laws are no physical fighting, no cheating on tests, and no drugs or alcohol.
>
> Last year, some students wanted more freedom. They hung a banner in the hall. It said, "Give us <u>liberty</u>!" The representatives then wrote a new rule. It was the Friday Half-Day Rule. On Fridays, students could go home at noon. The principal threw out the new rule. One student wrote to the school newspaper. He called the principal a <u>dictator</u>. The principal wrote a letter back. She said the high school is a <u>democracy</u> and that she is the president. She can <u>veto</u> laws passed by the student representatives!

**1.** constitution _____

_____

**2.** laws _____

_____

**3.** representatives _____

_____

**4.** election _____

_____

**5.** liberty _____

_____

**6.** dictator _____

_____

**7.** democracy _____

_____

**8.** veto _____

_____

Name _____  Date _____

 **1 ▶ Comparing Then and Now**          **Exercise 3**

**Below are some laws of ancient Rome. Our country today still follows three of
these laws. Mark these laws with an *X*.**

___  **1.** The man heads the family. All property is his.

___  **2.** It is legal to have slaves.

___  **3.** A man is accused of murder. He is innocent until proven guilty.

___  **4.** No person may hold a meeting at night in the city.

___  **5.** A person finds a horse. He takes it home. He is now the legal owner of the horse.

___  **6.** Women cannot plead innocent or guilty in court.

___  **7.** A neighbor's fruit falls on your land. You can pick it up.

___  **8.** A thief is caught stealing. He is whipped for his crime.

___  **9.** A man may divorce his wife. He then returns her to her family.

___  **10.** One person's tree blocks another's sunlight. The tree branches can be cut off.

**Now choose two of the laws you did not mark. Do you think they are good
laws or bad laws? Why do you think these laws are not followed today? On
the lines below, write a brief paragraph explaining your answer.**

_____

_____

_____

_____

_____

_____

_____

_____

_____

_____

# 2 ▶ Using a Code

By filling the blanks below with the correct words from the list, you will discover a code. Each number represents the letter above it. Using the code, complete the sentence at the bottom of the page.

| | | | |
|---|---|---|---|
| political | colony | charter | governors |
| freedom | direct democracy | contract | |

**1.** Having to do with matters of government

$\overline{\phantom{x}}\ \overline{\phantom{x}}\ \overline{\phantom{x}}\ \overline{\phantom{x}}\ \overline{\phantom{x}}\ \overline{\phantom{x}}\ \overline{\phantom{x}}\ \overline{\phantom{x}}\ \overline{\phantom{x}}$
1 12 15 4 30 4 18 5 15

**2.** A government in which every citizen votes on every matter

$\overline{\phantom{x}}\ \overline{\phantom{x}}\ \overline{\phantom{x}}\ \overline{\phantom{x}}\ \overline{\phantom{x}}\ \overline{\phantom{x}}\quad\overline{\phantom{x}}\ \overline{\phantom{x}}\ \overline{\phantom{x}}\ \overline{\phantom{x}}\ \overline{\phantom{x}}\ \overline{\phantom{x}}\ \overline{\phantom{x}}\ \overline{\phantom{x}}\ \overline{\phantom{x}}$
9 4 34 7 18 30    9 7 21 12 18 34 5 18 40

**3.** Liberty

$\overline{\phantom{x}}\ \overline{\phantom{x}}\ \overline{\phantom{x}}\ \overline{\phantom{x}}\ \overline{\phantom{x}}\ \overline{\phantom{x}}\ \overline{\phantom{x}}$
3 34 7 7 9 12 21

**4.** Land owned and governed by another country

$\overline{\phantom{x}}\ \overline{\phantom{x}}\ \overline{\phantom{x}}\ \overline{\phantom{x}}\ \overline{\phantom{x}}\ \overline{\phantom{x}}$
18 12 15 12 6 40

**5.** Any written statement of rights granted by a ruler or government

$\overline{\phantom{x}}\ \overline{\phantom{x}}\ \overline{\phantom{x}}\ \overline{\phantom{x}}\ \overline{\phantom{x}}\ \overline{\phantom{x}}\ \overline{\phantom{x}}$
18 2 5 34 30 7 34

**6.** People chosen by the king to rule over a colony

$\overline{\phantom{x}}\ \overline{\phantom{x}}\ \overline{\phantom{x}}\ \overline{\phantom{x}}\ \overline{\phantom{x}}\ \overline{\phantom{x}}\ \overline{\phantom{x}}\ \overline{\phantom{x}}\ \overline{\phantom{x}}$
19 12 8 7 34 6 12 34 20

**7.** A written agreement between two or more people

$\overline{\phantom{x}}\ \overline{\phantom{x}}\ \overline{\phantom{x}}\ \overline{\phantom{x}}\ \overline{\phantom{x}}\ \overline{\phantom{x}}\ \overline{\phantom{x}}\ \overline{\phantom{x}}$
18 12 6 30 34 5 18 30

Representatives of the First Continental Congress talked about more independence for the colonies. They wrote some of their thoughts down in a

$\overline{\phantom{x}}\ \overline{\phantom{x}}\ \overline{\phantom{x}}\ \overline{\phantom{x}}\ \overline{\phantom{x}}\ \overline{\phantom{x}}\ \overline{\phantom{x}}\ \overline{\phantom{x}}\ \overline{\phantom{x}}\ \overline{\phantom{x}}\ \overline{\phantom{x}}\quad\overline{\phantom{x}}\ \overline{\phantom{x}}\quad\overline{\phantom{x}}\ \overline{\phantom{x}}\ \overline{\phantom{x}}\ \overline{\phantom{x}}\ \overline{\phantom{x}}\ \overline{\phantom{x}}$
9 7 18 15 5 34 5 30 4 12 6    12 3    34 4 19 2 30 20

Name _____    Date _____

## 2 ▶ Debating an Issue                               **Exercise 5**

Not all the colonists wanted independence from Great Britain. Those who
did not were called Loyalists or Tories. Read the beginning of Adam's letter
to Sarah.

> Hartford, May 12, 1775
>
> Dear Sarah,
> Like you, I am upset by the talk of war. But I do not agree with
> you. I am a Loyalist. War is too high a price to pay for freedom.
> There are many good reasons to stay under British rule.

What do you think Adam's reasons are? Help organize a class debate on the
topic "Should the colonists break ties with Great Britain?"

**A.** On the lines below, list three arguments to support Adam's position of
remaining loyal to Great Britain.

1. _____

2. _____

3. _____

Now list three arguments in favor of independence from Great Britain.

1. _____

2. _____

3. _____

**B.** Now choose your position for the class debate. Ask your teacher to divide the
class into two groups: one group in favor of independence from Great Britain
and one group against it. Allow each group member 3–5 minutes to present
the group's position, and continue taking turns until each member of the
group has spoken. Vote on whether or not to declare independence. You may
review Chapter 2 in your textbook to help you complete this exercise.

# 2 ▶ Composing a National Anthem

**Exercise 6**

*Critical Thinking*

Congress approved the Declaration of Independence in 1776. However, our national anthem was not written until 1814. In that year, America was again at war with Great Britain. A young lawyer, Francis Scott Key, was held prisoner on a British warship in the harbor of Baltimore, Maryland.

One night, Key watched the bombing of a fort. He wrote a poem on a scrap of paper. He called the poem "The Star-Spangled Banner." Later, the poem was made into a song. The song did not become the national anthem until 1931!

Below are the first lines of "The Star-Spangled Banner." Read them. Think about what your country means to you and your fellow citizens today. Then try writing your own national anthem on the lines below.

> O say, can you see, by the dawn's early light,
> What so proudly we hail'd at the twilight's last gleaming?
> Whose broad stripes and bright stars, thro' the perilous fight,
> O'er the ramparts we watch'd, were so gallantly streaming?

_____

_____

_____

_____

_____

_____

_____

_____

_____

_____

_____

## 2 ▶ Rewriting History

Self-government in the colonies began in 1619. However, the colonies did not break ties with Great Britain until 1776. In that year, Thomas Jefferson wrote the Declaration of Independence. A new government was established when Congress accepted the Declaration of Independence on July 4, 1776. That government has lasted more than 200 years.

What if the story of our country had turned out differently? Suppose the Second Continental Congress had rejected the Declaration of Independence. What do you think our history would have been like? Would the country still have expanded westward all the way to the Pacific Ocean? Would there have been a Civil War? How many of Britain's wars would the colonies have had to support with soldiers and money?

On the lines below, write a brief essay describing what life would have been like in America for the past 200 years if the colonies had not broken their ties with Great Britain.

_____

_____

_____

_____

_____

_____

_____

_____

_____

_____

_____

# 3 ▶ Dramatizing an Event

**Exercise 8**

**With your class, dramatize the Constitutional Convention of 1787. Do the following:**

1. Elect a president for the convention. In 1787, the president was George Washington. He ran the convention and kept order among the delegates. Your president will do the same.

2. As a delegate, you will pick a colony to represent. Research your colony. Which issues were important to that colony in 1787?

3. Are you a Federalist or an anti-Federalist? Choose one. Be prepared to argue your position.

4. Decide whether you are willing to make compromises at the Constitutional Convention.

5. These issues may come up at your convention. Where do you stand on them?
   - slave trade
   - export taxes
   - a strong national government

6. Pick an idea from the Magna Carta that you want in the Constitution.

7. There were 40 delegates at the convention. Elect as many delegates as your class has students. (Remember—this is no longer 1787. Electing women and minority delegates is allowed.)

**Use the space below for your notes.**

Name _____  Date _____

The map below shows the thirteen original states at the time of the
Constitutional Convention. Use the map to answer the questions.

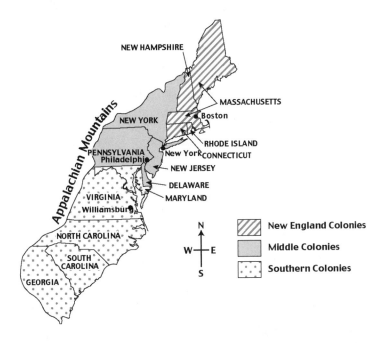

1. Alexander Hamilton was a delegate from New York. In which direction did he go from his home to the convention in Philadelphia?

   _____

2. At the convention, the southern delegates wanted slaves counted as part of their population. Name two states that favored this idea.

   _____

3. The northern delegates were against slaves being counted. Name two states that opposed counting slaves as part of a state's population.

   _____

4. Name the states that the delegate from Georgia passed on the way to Philadelphia.

   _____

5. What are the two major cities that are located north of where the convention was held?

   _____

# 3 ▶ Writing a Journal Entry

**Exercise 10**

*Critical Thinking*

A journal is a private diary of someone's thoughts and feelings. You are a delegate to the Constitutional Convention. On the lines below, write a journal entry about one day at the convention. Use the information in your textbook, or look at an encyclopedia or other reference book for more facts about the convention. Use the questions below to help you prepare your entry.

• How quickly is the Constitution being written?

• What compromises are being made? How do you feel about the compromises?

• Are the delegates getting along?

• Has anything happened that makes you angry?

• Are you glad you came?

• Do you feel the delegates, including yourself, really represent the people?

• How do you think you would feel about the convention if you were not a delegate?

_____

_____

_____

_____

_____

_____

_____

_____

_____

_____

_____

_____

_____

Name _____     Date _____

 **3 ▶ Identifying Fact and Opinion**                    **Exercise 11**

> It is September 18, 1787. The delegates to the Constitutional Convention had just signed the Constitution the day before in Philadelphia's Independence Hall. Outside on the street, two men are talking. One is a Philadelphia merchant. The other is a farmer from Delaware.

**Read the conversation below. Then write an *F* for fact or an *O* for opinion on the lines following their statements.**

**Farmer:** Those delegates were in there for months! _____ That's too long! I guess some people don't need to work. _____

**Merchant:** My business would go bust if I were away that long! _____ I just hope the government is going to raise some money. _____

**Farmer:** Money! I don't want the national government collecting taxes. _____ I say, let the states raise their own money. _____

**Merchant:** Some states are collecting taxes. _____ It's a mess. Pennsylvania is taxing goods crossing through the state. _____ Prices are going up too much. _____

**Farmer:** What did the delegates decide about representatives? My state of Delaware is small. _____ We should have the same number of representatives as the larger states. _____ That's only fair. _____

**Merchant:** No, each state should have representatives based on population. _____

**News Reporter (passing by):** You both win! The delegates compromised and each state will send two representatives to the Senate. _____

**Farmer:** A Senate is a great idea. _____

**News Reporter:** But James Madison had this plan. The House will have representatives based on each state's population. _____

**Merchant:** The House is an even better idea! _____

# 4 ▶ Completing a Chart

Create an amendment chart using the form below. In the left-hand column, write the first six amendments to the Constitution. Then write the letter of each real-life situation listed below in the right-hand column next to the amendment to which it applies. You may review Chapter 4 in your textbook to copy the six amendments.

| Amendment | Situation |
|---|---|
|  |  |
|  |  |
|  |  |
|  |  |
|  |  |
|  |  |

**A.** Carol Lawson is accused of robbing a bank. She says she is innocent. Carol does not think the trial judge will give her a fair hearing. She asks for a jury trial.

**B.** Does Jason have stolen goods in his car? The police want to know. They want to search his car. Yet, they cannot. He will not let them. They do not have a search warrant.

**C.** Ramona's father keeps a gun under his bed. Ramona does not like it. He says he needs it to protect the family. He also says that it is his right to own a gun.

**D.** Mrs. Wong goes to her own church. Her neighbors do not like her church. They think Mrs. Wong's religion is strange. However, Mrs. Wong does as she likes. Choosing her own religion is her right.

**E.** Someone killed the mayor of Newton. Jerome Smith hated the mayor. Everyone knows it. Jerome is arrested for the crime. He is never brought to trial because no one saw the murder. Jerome's friend says Jerome was with him at the time. The grand jury cannot find enough evidence against Jerome.

Name _____  Date _____

 **4** ▶ **Creating a Chart**                          **Exercise 13**

*Critical Thinking*

Extend your amendment chart. Add five other amendments of your choice.
Write them in the left-hand column. Listen to the news. Check the newspapers
for a few days. Find more real-life situations that apply to the five amendments.
Place the situations in the right-hand column on the chart.

| Amendment | Situations |
|---|---|
|  |  |
|  |  |
|  |  |
|  |  |
|  |  |

# 4 ▶ Writing a Grievance Letter

**Exercise 14**

*Critical Thinking*

The Declaration of Independence has three sections. The second section is the grievances against the king of Great Britain. The men who wrote the grievances were doing something brave. They were criticizing the king. In the colonies, freedom of speech was not yet a right. Freedom of speech became the First Amendment to the Constitution. Today, Americans are free to criticize the government or the President.

Read the grievances in the Declaration of Independence. Think about what grievances or complaints you have heard people make against our government. Look at the editorial page of the newspaper. The newspaper editors write their opinions on this page. Other people's letters or articles are printed there, too. Many are complaints about our government. Choose one. Attach it to this page. Then think of something that makes you angry or displeased about our government. It could be our federal government or your state or local government. On the lines below, write a brief letter detailing your grievances against the government.

_____

_____

_____

_____

_____

_____

_____

_____

_____

_____

_____

# 5 ▶ Questioning Your Representative

**Exercise 15**

*Critical Thinking*

Your congressional representative is often in Washington D.C. This is where the representatives work. Each representative also keeps a local office. If the representative is away, aides meet with constituents. Later, the aides tell the representatives about their constituents' views and concerns.

   Your representative or one of his or her aides is visiting your class. Fill out the form below so you are ready for the visit.

Your representative's name: _____

Address of local office: _____

Phone number of local office: _____

**A.** Write some questions you might ask the visitor about the following issues:

**1.** Jobs _____

_____

_____

**2.** Health care _____

_____

_____

**3.** Taxes _____

_____

_____

**4.** Crime _____

_____

_____

**B.** Now write to your representative's office. Ask about a bill your representative is sponsoring. Ask the office to send your class information about the bill. Then decide how you feel about it. On a separate sheet of paper, write a brief essay either for or against the bill. Give reasons for your answer.

# 5 ▶ Writing a Political Commercial

**Exercise 16**

*Critical Thinking*

Congress is voting on a bill. This bill is about buying guns. Under the new law, a person who has been convicted of any crime would never be able to buy a gun.

When Congress is considering a new law, there are often radio and television commercials or newspaper ads for or against such bills. They ask people to call or write members of Congress. Sometimes, these commercials play on people's fears. Here are two examples of openings for radio commercials. They are both about the proposed gun bill.

---

**AGAINST:**

America is a free country. Let's keep it that way. Lawmakers are trying to take away your freedoms. The gun bill would take away your freedom to buy what you want. It would take away store owners' freedom to sell what they want. America is the land of liberty. Let's keep it that way!

**FOR:**

Right this minute a man, woman, or child is being shot! Many crimes committed with guns are committed by people who have already been convicted of a crime. This new gun bill could help dramatically reduce shootings by keeping guns out of the hands of known criminals. This bill would help save people's lives!

---

Check your newspaper for a few days. Find a story about a new bill that Congress is considering. Then, on the lines below, write your own radio or television commercial either for or against the bill.

_____

_____

_____

_____

_____

_____

_____

_____

# 5 ▶ Role-Playing a Senator's Aide                      Exercise 17

*Critical Thinking*

You work as a senator's aide. (A senator's aide is someone who studies the issues the senator is concerned with and gives him or her advice.) The Senate is considering a bill on open grazing. Right now, farmers can graze their cattle on government lands. They do not pay the government. However, the new law would change that. Farmers would have to pay money for grazing rights on a per-cow basis.

> A local farmer said, "This bill will ruin my ranch. I can't afford to pay money to graze my cows."
>
> A local environmentalist said, "The cattle should not graze on government land at all. They destroy the land for other plants and animals. Besides, beef isn't healthy to eat. I support this bill. Let's stop raising so many cattle."
>
> A local business owner said, "This bill worries me. The farmers sell their beef to me. Then I sell it in my supermarket chains. If this bill passes, the farmers will charge me more. Then I'll have to charge my customers more. But will they still buy beef?"

What would you recommend to Senator Jimenez about the grazing bill? Should she support it or not? On the lines below, write a brief essay explaining your position. Give reasons for your recommendation.

_____

_____

_____

_____

_____

_____

_____

# 6 ▶ Making a Timeline

## Exercise 18

*Skill Practice*

Bills in Congress can take a long time to get passed. Sometimes, a bill can be in committees for the whole legislative session. At the end of the two years, if there is no action on the bill, it dies. The representative sponsoring the bill has to rewrite it for the next session.

Contact your representative's office. Ask for the recent history of two bills the representative sponsored in the last year. (Ask for bills that made it out of committee and were voted on by Congress.) Place those bills on a timeline in the space below. Add the months and dates of the various stages the bill went through before Congress voted on it. Then add a new bill your representative is sponsoring this year. Track this bill on the timeline throughout the year by reading your local newspaper or contacting the representative's office from time to time.

Name _____ Date _____

 **6 ▷ Using a Chart**                    **Exercise 19**

Look at the topics on the chart below. Follow the newspapers, or listen to the
TV or radio news. Watch for bills Congress is considering on the topics. Then
write a summary of at least one bill across from each topic on the chart.

| Topic | Bill |
|---|---|
| Jobs | |
| Health Care | |
| Crime | |
| Military | |
| Environment | |

# 6 ▶ Passing a New Law

**Exercise 20**

*Critical Thinking*

Your class is the Congress. One member wants to introduce a new bill. This bill would limit the school year to six months. All students would then have to work the other six months of the year.

Follow the steps below to take the bill through the different stages so that it can become a law. You might choose just one of the steps to demonstrate.

**Step 1:** Bring a box to class. This box is the hopper for bills. Assign two students (a House sponsor and a Senate sponsor) to describe the bill on a piece of paper. Give the bill a short title and a number. Make copies of the bill for your class. Drop the bill in the hopper.

**Step 2:** Form a standing committee of five students. Have the two sponsors talk about the bill to the committee. Ask any students who oppose the bill to speak to the committee as well. Then ask the committee to vote on the bill.

**Step 3:** Now have half the class (the Senate) debate the bill. The Senate sponsor will speak in favor of the bill to the full group. After the bill has been debated, the Senate might make changes to it. Then have the full Senate vote on and pass the bill. Write the bill as it now is, including any changes.

**Step 4:** The bill now goes to the House (the other half of the class). Have the House sponsor lead the House debate on the bill. The House might make more changes to the bill. Then have the House vote.

**Step 5:** Pick a conference committee. It should have three members each from both the House and the Senate. This committee will meet in secret. It will work out problems between the House and Senate versions of the bill. Then have the committee read the bill to the entire class. The whole class (House and Senate) will then vote on the bill.

**Step 6:** Ask your teacher to be the President. Send your bill to the President. Did he or she sign it? If so, the bill is now law. If the teacher vetoes the bill, the class can then try to pass it again. If two-thirds of the entire class votes in favor of the bill, you have overridden the President's veto. The bill is now law.

# 6 ▸ Summarizing a Proposed Bill

**Exercise 21**

*Review*

This is one page of an actual proposed bill. (The whole bill was over 150 pages long!) A California Congressperson wanted a law that would provide Americans with proper health care. Most propsed bills are very long. Sometimes, it is hard for members of Congress to read every page of each bill. To help them quickly learn about all the proposed bills, the *Congressional Record* prints a summary of them.

Read the page from the health care bill below. Key words are in italics for you. Use the key words to summarize the section of the bill on the lines below.

**99th Congress**
**1st Session**
**H.R. 2049**

*To establish a United States Health Service to provide high quality health care and to overcome the deficiencies in the present system of health care delivery.*

The *right* to be accompanied and *visited* at any time by a friend, relative, or independent advocate of the individual's choosing, and the *right* to have routine *services*, such as feeding, bathing, dressing, and bedding changes, performed *by a friend or relative,* if the individual so chooses.

The *right* in the event of *terminal illness,* to *die* with a maximum degree of *dignity,* to be provided all necessary symptom *relief,* to be provided (and for the individual's family to be provided) *counseling* and *comfort,* and to be allowed (if desired) to *die at home.*

_____

_____

_____

_____

_____

_____

_____

_____

_____

_____

# 7 ▷ Describing an Event

**Exercise 22**

*Skill Practice*

One of the most important events in the President's life is the inauguration. On Inauguration Day, the President is sworn into office. The President then makes a speech outlining goals and visions for the country. After that, there is often a parade. That night, there are balls and parties for the new President, the Vice President, and their families.

Today, much of the President's inauguration can be seen on television. You might have watched an inauguration. If so, on the lines below, write a few paragraphs describing what it was like. Or ask some older members of your family about an inauguration they remember. Describe what they tell you.

You can also read through a book about one of our past Presidents and get information about that inauguration. Write a description of what took place.

_____

_____

_____

_____

_____

_____

_____

_____

_____

_____

_____

_____

_____

_____

_____

Name _____ Date _____

In 1789, the Senate held a hot debate. It was led by Senator Maclay of Pennsylvania. The senator had been to a big party for the new President, George Washington. Senator Maclay was from the frontier. He lived a simple life. He thought big parties cost too much. He called them "fopperies."

Today, we hold even bigger inaugural celebrations — three or four days of balls, parades, and expensive dinners, all surrounding the swearing in of the new President.

Many people today feel much as Senator Maclay did in 1789. They think large inauguration parties are a waste of a lot of money. They feel that the money could be put to better use for things that Americans need. However, others feel that the inauguration of a new President is such a special event that it deserves a big celebration.

How do you feel? On the lines below, write a brief essay explaining why we should or should not hold a big inaugural celebration when a new President takes office.

_____

_____

_____

_____

_____

_____

_____

_____

_____

_____

●

## 7 ▷ Diagramming the President's Duties

**Exercise 24**

*Skill Practice*

Below is a diagram of the various roles of the President. Complete the diagram
by filling in the different duties the President performs in each of those roles.
You may review Chapter 7 in your textbook if you need to.

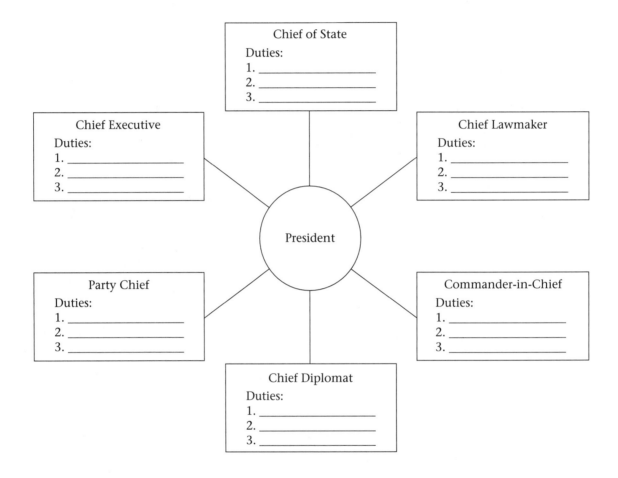

Name _____   Date _____

## 7 ▶ Charting the Roles of the President          **Exercise 25**

*Critical Thinking*

Look at the chart below. The left-hand column lists the six major roles of the
President. Read the newspapers every day for a few weeks. Clip out stories
about the President that describe him fulfilling each of these roles. Then write
a two- or three-sentence summary of each article in the appropriate place
opposite each role.

| Role | Description |
|---|---|
| Chief Executive | |
| Chief of State | |
| Chief Lawmaker | |
| Chief Diplomat | |
| Commander-in-Chief | |
| Party Chief | |

# 8 ▷ Solving Government Problems                    Exercise 26

Each day, our government is faced with many problems. Read the situations below. Each one is a real problem our government has faced recently. Choose a department that would handle each situation from the list below. Write the letter of that department beside the problem.

___ **1.** China takes away its people's rights without good reason. Should we punish China and stop trading with it?

___ **2.** The President wants free vaccine shots for all children. However, many of the drug companies object because it is costly.

___ **3.** The government is shutting down dozens of army bases. What will the empty bases be used for? What will happen to the communities where the bases are located?

___ **4.** The head of this department is meeting with important people from other countries. They are talking about world economic problems. They discuss countries borrowing money from each other. They talk about customs, duties, and taxes.

___ **5.** There is a horrible war going on in Bosnia. Innocent people are being killed, and many more are starving. Our country wants to help.

___ **6.** The delta smelt is a small fish. Few of them are left in California. People are taking too much water, and the fish do not have enough to survive.

___ **7.** The government is thinking about cutting farm subsidies. Many congressional representatives from farm states complain to this department that this policy would hurt their constituents.

___ **8.** Many students cannot afford to attend college. Yet, they should be able to get an education. One idea is having students take part in community service in exchange for college fees.

___ **9.** A religious cult has accumulated a large number of illegal weapons. The government wants to break up the group and arrest its leader.

___ **10.** The country needs more money. The President suggests a gas tax. The oil companies are against it.

**a.** Department of the Treasury

**b.** Department of Education

**c.** Department of the Interior

**d.** Department of Justice

**e.** Department of Agriculture

**f.** Department of State

**g.** Department of Commerce

**h.** Department of Defense

**i.** Department of Energy

**j.** Department of Health and Human Services

# 8 ▶ Brainstorming an Executive Department

**Exercise 27**

*Critical Thinking*

Some of the executive departments have been around since our federal government was first established. The three oldest are the Departments of State, Treasury, and War. (War is now the Defense Department.) In 1789, President Washington found that these three departments were necessary. Treasury printed money for the new country. War organized an army. State handled foreign relations.

Other departments were established later to meet certain needs. For example, the Department of Energy was set up in 1977 by President Carter. At that time, our country bought its oil from Middle Eastern countries. However, those countries kept cutting their production of oil. Suddenly, there was a shortage of foreign oil in the United States. The new Department of Energy was set up to help the United States become less dependent on foreign oil.

A new executive department has been formed at your school. It is the Department of Fairness and Safety. Brainstorm with other students. Come up with ideas for the new department. What is the department's role? What issues will it deal with? Have a recorder write the ideas on the board. Then use the ideas to fill in the chart below.

| Department of Fairness and Safety | |
|---|---|
| **Role** | **Issues** |
| | |

Name _____          Date _____

You have been offered a job with the federal government. You have a good
background in several areas, so you can choose a position with any of the
government agencies listed below. Think about the responsibilities of each
of these agencies. Then choose a job in one of them. Write a brief essay
telling what job you have chosen, why you chose it, and what duties and
responsibilities you are looking forward to performing. (You may review pages
101–111 in your textbook if you need to.)

Department of Justice
Department of Interior
Department of Housing and Urban Development
NASA
EPA
ACTION

_____

_____

_____

_____

_____

_____

_____

_____

_____

_____

_____

_____

_____

_____

Name _____ Date _____

Look at the Venn diagrams below. In the center of each one are the responsibilities of more than one department or agency. The agencies and departments are listed below. Complete the diagram by writing the names of the departments and agencies in the correct circles. You may review Chapter 8 in your textbook if you need help.

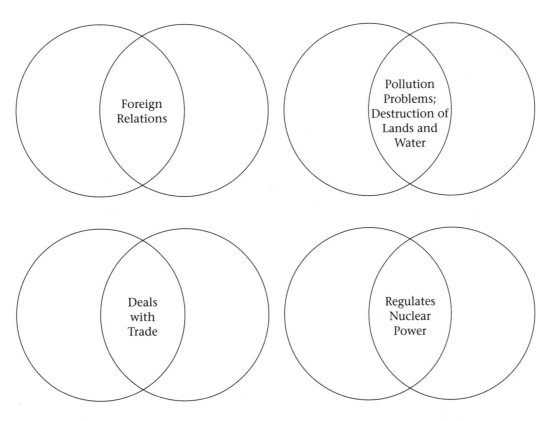

Environmental Protection Agency      Department of the Interior

Department of State      Department of Energy

ACTION      Federal Trade Commission

Department of Commerce      Nuclear Regulatory Commission

Name_____     Date_____

# 9 ▶ Identifying the Federal Courts

Read the sentences below. Decide whether each one describes either a U.S. District Court, a U.S. Court of Appeal, or the U.S. Supreme Court. Write *DC* for District Court, *CA* for Court of Appeal, or *SC* for Supreme Court next to each statement.

____ **1.** This court is the highest court in the land.

____ **2.** This court is one of 91 courts spread across the country.

____ **3.** Each state in the union has at least one of these courts.

____ **4.** This court and others like it are spread across the country in circuits.

____ **5.** Nine justices hear cases on this court.

____ **6.** People accused of bank robbery and kidnapping are tried in this court.

____ **7.** This court has only appellate jurisdiction.

____ **8.** The number of judges on this court ranges from 3 to 15.

____ **9.** This court can hear only two kinds of cases in original jurisdiction.

____ **10.** Sometimes a three-judge panel may hear a case on this court.

Name _____ Date _____

# 9 ▶ Profiling a Supreme Court Justice

## Exercise 31

*Skill Practice*

Use an encyclopedia, other reference book, or the Internet to research one of the U.S. Supreme Court justices listed in the box. Read the information about that justice. Then use that information to complete the profile below.

| | |
|---|---|
| John Jay | Earl Warren |
| John Marshall | William Brennan |
| Oliver Wendell Holmes | Thurgood Marshall |
| Louis D. Brandeis | Sandra Day O'Connor |

## Supreme Court Justice Profile

Name of justice: _____

Birthdate: _____

Birthplace: _____

Home state: _____

School background: _____

_____

Important work before serving on Supreme Court: _____

_____

Year appointed to Supreme Court: _____

Appointed by President: _____

Key decisions/opinions while on the Supreme Court: _____

_____

_____

Year retired from the Supreme Court: _____

Any other interesting facts about this justice: _____

_____

# 9 ▶ Classifying Federal Court Cases

**Exercise 32**

*Skill Practice*

Read through your city's newspaper for a two- or three-week period. Clip out as many stories about federal court cases as you can find. Read through the stories. Write a brief paragraph that explains what the case was about. Then write the summary on the chart below next to the appropriate court that decided the case.

| Court | Cases |
|---|---|
| U.S. District Court | |
| U.S. Court of Appeals | |
| U.S. Supreme Court | |

# 10 ▷ Identifying State Capitals                          **Exercise 33**

The United States has been settled by many different groups of people. The names of many U.S. cities often reflect the group that settled there. Here are the names of ten state capitals. Below the names is information about the origin of each capital. Write the letter of the capital next to the statement that describes the origin of its name.

**a.** Tallahassee, Florida          **f.** Jefferson City, Missouri

**b.** Baton Rouge, Louisiana     **g.** Harrisburg, Pennsylvania

**c.** Annapolis, Maryland          **h.** Pierre, South Dakota

**d.** Santa Fe, New Mexico       **i.** St. Paul, Minnesota

**e.** Little Rock, Arkansas        **j.** Cheyenne, Wyoming

_____ **1.** This capital was named by the Spanish colonists. It was first named La Villa Real de la Santa Fe. In Spanish, these words mean "the royal city of the holy faith."

_____ **2.** This capital name means "Anne's city." It was named after Queen Anne of England. Queen Anne gave the city its charter in 1708.

_____ **3.** Major Dodge, doing work on the railroad, named this city after the Cheyenne Indians living there.

_____ **4.** This capital means "red stick" in French. A red stick was stuck in the ground when explorers came. The stick was the line between two Indian nations.

_____ **5.** Pierre Chouteau was an early fur trader. He settled this town in 1878. It later became a state capital.

_____ **6.** This capital was named after an Apalachee Indian word meaning "old town" or "abandoned fields." Spanish settlers found an abandoned Indian village there.

_____ **7.** This town was named for one of our Presidents. The President was also one of our country's founders.

_____ **8.** John Harris, Sr., ran the ferry. His son laid out a town in 1785. The family gave the land to the state. The town later became the capital. The capital is named after the family.

_____ **9.** This capital was settled in 1840 by several families and a French trader. The trader's name was Pierre Parrant, but his nickname was Pig's Eye. The town was called Pig's Eye. In 1841, the families built a church. The church was named for St. Paul. The town was renamed after the church.

_____ **10.** In 1772, a French explorer went down the Arkansas River. There were hills over the river. The explorer called the hills "La Petite Roche." These French words mean "the little rock."

# 10 ▶ Identifying Correct Information

One of a state's most important powers is the power to set its own rules and regulations for driving. Each state has its own department of motor vehicles (DMV), which sets guidelines and regulations for driver's licenses and vehicle registration. Every state DMV puts out its own driver's handbook. Get a copy of your state's driver's handbook from your local DMV. Use it to answer the questions below.

**1.** Who must have a license to drive in your state?

_____

**2.** How old must a person be to get a driving permit?

_____

**3.** What is needed to register a car?

_____

**4.** What are your state's laws on drinking and driving?

_____

**5.** Name three rights that pedestrians have in your state.

_____

_____

**6.** Name three of your state's speed limit laws.

_____

_____

**7.** What are two illegal uses of a driver's license in your state?

_____

_____

**8.** List two new driving laws you think your state should have.

_____

_____

Name _____ Date _____

**Use what you know about the powers of the states to complete the crossword puzzle.**

DOWN
**States can:**

2. issue _____ for drivers

3. establish _____ for young people

4. set up their own _____ (s) where people vote for officials

8. issue licenses for professionals such

as _____

10. set the _____ for learning to drive or for getting married

ACROSS
**States cannot:**

1. enter into a foreign _____ or treaty

5. grant titles of _____

6. print _____

7. engage in _____ (s)

9. _____ their own armies

11. establish _____ limits for roads and highways

# 10 ▶ Planning a School Menu

In 1943, the federal government put out important information about nutrition. The government recommended that people should eat certain foods from different food groups each day. These food groups were called RDAs.

States still use the RDA lists today. They use them to decide what foods must be served in places such as schools, day-care centers, nursing homes, and hospitals.

Over the years, the federal government has changed the RDA list of basic foods. The most recent change came in 1992. When the federal government changes the RDA, states must change their rules and regulations. Look at the pyramid of food groups issued in 1992.

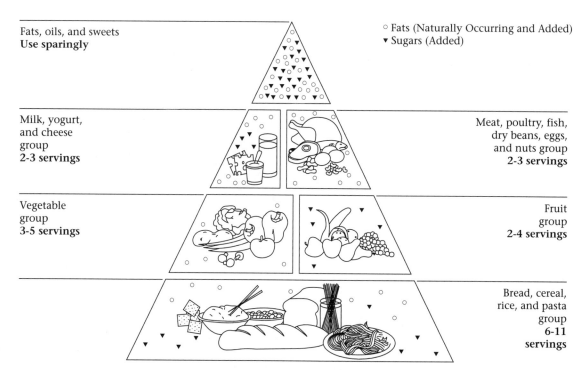

Fats, oils, and sweets
**Use sparingly**

○ Fats (Naturally Occurring and Added)
▼ Sugars (Added)

Milk, yogurt, and cheese group
**2-3 servings**

Meat, poultry, fish, dry beans, eggs, and nuts group
**2-3 servings**

Vegetable group
**3-5 servings**

Fruit group
**2-4 servings**

Bread, cereal, rice, and pasta group
**6-11 servings**

Source: U.S. Department of Agriculture, U.S, Department of Health and Human Services

# 10 ▷ Planning a School Menu (continued)　　　Exercise 36

**A.** You are a state health worker assigned to set up a school lunch program. Use the chart below to conduct a taste test survey in your class. Ask ten students in class which foods they would like to have on a school lunch menu. Circle the first letter of the kind of food that each student chooses in the column marked "Student preference."

| Food group | Items | Student preference |
|:---:|:---:|:---:|
| I | Bread, pasta, or rice | B B B B B B B B B B<br>P P P P P P P P P P<br>R R R R R R R R R R |
| II | Apples, bananas, or oranges | A A A A A A A A A A<br>B B B B B B B B B B<br>O O O O O O O O O O |
| III | Broccoli, spinach, or carrots | B B B B B B B B B B<br>S S S S S S S S S S<br>C C C C C C C C C C |
| IV | Meat, fish, or poultry | M M M M M M M M M M<br>F F F F F F F F F F<br>P P P P P P P P P P |
| V | Milk, cheese, or yogurt | M M M M M M M M M M<br>C C C C C C C C C C<br>Y Y Y Y Y Y Y Y Y Y |
| VI | Fats, oils, or sweets | No amount recommended |

**B.** Now use the information you collected to write a lunch menu for your school for three days. Write your menu on the lines below.

_____

_____

_____

_____

_____

Name_____ Date_____

# 11 ▸ Identifying State Ballot Proposals

**A.** In Chapter 11 of your textbook, you learned about three types of state ballot proposals: referendums, initiatives, and recalls. Look at the statements below. Decide whether each one describes an initiative (I), a referendum (R), or a recall (RC). Write the correct letter or letters on the line next to each statement. You may review Chapter 11 if you need to.

1. The people of a state want a tough new law to control toxic waste in their towns. They sign a petition for the law, and it is placed on the ballot at the next

   election. _____

2. A state legislature is considering a law that will allow tolls on all state highways. The people sign a petition to stop the legislature from acting. The proposed law is

   placed on the ballot at the next election for the voters to decide. _____

3. The citizens of a city believe their mayor is doing a poor job. Many people sign a petition to remove the mayor from office. A new election is held to find out whether

   the mayor can remain in office or will be replaced by another person. _____

4. A state legislature passes a law that allows cities around the state to tax movie theater admissions. The law has not gone into effect yet. The people sign a petition, and the

   proposed law has to be voted on in the next general statewide election. _____

**B.** Think about some law that you would like to see passed in your state. Or perhaps you have read about a law that your state legislature is considering that you oppose. On another sheet of paper, write a draft of either an initiative or a referendum for some kind of legislation that you either are in favor of or oppose. Then see how many of your classmates you can get to sign your draft. If you can get more than 75 percent of your class to sign it, send the document to your local state representative (if your state has either of these types of ballots). Your idea could even make it all the way to the ballot in your next statewide election!

Name_____  Date_____

 **11** ▸ **Conducting an Initiative/Referendum Campaign**   **Exercise 38**

In Chapter 11 on page 150, you read about an example of an initiative. It was a tough new law against drunk drivers. States allowing initiatives often have heated campaigns before elections. Usually, people feel strongly about initiatives and referendums, either for them or against them. Groups often raise money to air radio and TV commercials, run newspaper ads, or put up billboard posters.

On the lines below, write the commercial or advertising text for the initiative or referendum you drafted in Part B of Exercise 37. Or on a separate sheet of paper, draw a poster for that same initiative or referendum.

_____

_____

_____

_____

_____

_____

_____

_____

_____

_____

_____

_____

# 11 ▶ Evaluating a Poster or an Ad

**Exercise 39**

*Critical Thinking*

As you know, groups often wage heavy campaigns for and against state initiatives. They air radio and TV commercials, run newspaper ads, and put up billboards and posters in support of or in opposition to initiatives.

**A.** Find a campaign ad, poster, or billboard for or against a state initiative. Attach a copy of it to this page, or describe it below. Then give it a rating using the chart below.

---

**Rating Chart**

10 points—bad, won't work!
20 points—needs something more
30—OK, but not great
40—almost there
50—A winner! Really gets the message across

---

**B.** Now write a paragraph or two about the ad you chose. Tell why you rated it as you did.

_____

_____

_____

_____

_____

_____

_____

_____

_____

_____

Name_____ Date_____

# 11 ▶ Tracking a State Bill

**Exercise 40**

**A.** Find out the name of your state assembly or state senate representative. You can learn the name by calling your public library or looking on the Internet. Look up your representative in the phone book. Phone his or her office and ask what bills your representative is sponsoring. Ask the representative's aide to suggest a bill you can profile and track. Ask to have a computer printout of the bill sent to you. Once you receive the printout, complete the information below.

**1.** The name of the bill and a brief history of how the representative came to sponsor it:

_____

_____

**2.** A summary of the bill:

_____

_____

_____

**3.** The bill's current status (what is happening to the bill right now):

_____

_____

**4.** Ask your friends and family how they feel about this bill. Describe the reactions of two or three people to this bill possibly becoming law.

_____

_____

_____

**B.** Call your representative's office each week, and keep track of what is happening to the bill. If the bill comes to a final vote, circle the result of that vote here. My representative's bill (became law/failed to pass).

## 12 ▸ Describing an Event                    **Exercise 41**

*Critical Thinking*

Sixteen of our Presidents were once state governors. Because running a state government is in many ways like running the federal government, governors are often a natural choice for President.

Below is a true story about a governor. This governor later served as President longer than any other President in history.

---

In 1924, a friend asked Franklin D. Roosevelt to make a speech for him. Roosevelt's friend was running for the Democratic nomination for President. This friend wanted Roosevelt to nominate him at the Democratic convention that year. However, there was a problem. Roosevelt could not walk. Three years before, he had contracted polio. This terrible disease had left him in a wheelchair. Yet he agreed to make the speech anyway. So there he sat in his wheelchair at the Democratic convention. Hundreds of delegates were waiting. How would Roosevelt get up on the stage? Would he have to be carried?

Roosevelt's name was called as the next speaker. He rose very slowly from his wheelchair. He took hold of his crutches. Then he dragged himself along, step by step, to the stage. He pulled himself up the steps to the speaker's stand. No one said a word. Then Roosevelt grinned and waved. Everyone rose and cheered wildly. On that day, Franklin Roosevelt began the political comeback that, eight years later, would result in his being elected the thirty-second President of the United States.

---

You are a reporter. On a separate sheet of paper, write a news story about this event as though you were there. Describe what happened. You also have inside information. You have been told that Roosevelt is thinking of running for governor in 1928. Describe how the events of the convention might affect his campaign for governor four years later. If you need more information about this period of Roosevelt's life, you may check an encyclopedia or the Internet. Use the lines below to make some notes before you write your story.

_____

_____

_____

_____

_____

Name _____    Date _____

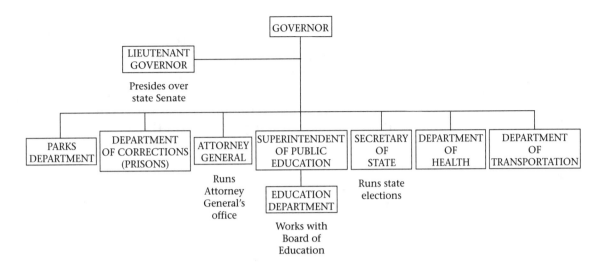

The chart above shows how most state governments are run. Compare this chart with the one on page 112 of your textbook. Use the charts to answer the questions below.

**1.** Which state position is most like that of the Vice President?

_____

**2.** Name four state departments that are found at the federal level.

_____

_____

**3.** Name four executive federal departments that are not found on the state level.

_____

_____

**4.** Write a brief paragraph explaining why serving as a state governor should be good preparation for being President.

_____

_____

_____

_____

## 12 ▶ Writing a Letter to the Governor

**Exercise 43**

*Critical Thinking*

Is there something in your state that especially pleases you? Or is there something that especially bothers you? Write your governor a letter. In the letter, tell the governor exactly how you feel about living in your state. Describe things you like and things you do not like. You may make suggestions about ways to change some of the things you do not like. Use the form and the lines below to write your letter. (If you are not sure of the name and address of your governor, contact your local library or look on the Internet.)

The Honorable _____

Governor of _____

(address) _____

(city, state, zip code) _____

Dear Governor,

_____

_____

_____

_____

_____

_____

_____

_____

Sincerely,

_____ (Sign your name)

_____ (Print or type your name)

**13** **Questioning a Public Defender** **Exercise 44**

You read about a man named Clarence Gideon in your textbook. You know that the court chose a lawyer for Gideon. This kind of lawyer is called a public defender. A public defender is a lawyer appointed by the courts to defend someone who cannot afford to pay for his or her own private attorney.

Look in your phone book. Find the county government office listings. Look up the Public Defender's office. It might be listed this way:

> Public Defender
> Superior Court Division
> Investigation Division
> Juvenile Division

Have the class contact the Public Defender's Juvenile Division. Ask that a speaker from the office come and talk to the class. Think about questions you might ask the speaker. Here is one question people are often curious about:

What if the public defender knows the accused is guilty? How can he or she defend a guilty person?

List five other questions for the guest speaker below.

1. _____

   _____

2. _____

   _____

3. _____

   _____

4. _____

   _____

5. _____

   _____

If a speaker cannot visit your class, write or e-mail a letter to the office and include your questions. Ask someone at the office to send you a reply.

# 13 ▶ Defining Words

Below are some of the Words to Know from Chapter 13 in your textbook. Find articles in your newspaper that contain sentences with these words. Write the sentences on the lines below. Then use the words in sentences of your own on the lines that follow.

*assault* _____

_____

Your sentence: _____

_____

*intoxicated* _____

_____

Your sentence: _____

_____

*witnesses* _____

_____

Your sentence: _____

_____

*deadlocked* _____

_____

Your sentence: _____

_____

# 14 ▶ Creating a Trash Sculpture

**Exercise 46**

*Critical Thinking*

Disposing of trash is a local problem all communities have. Most communities have groups that organize waste recycling.

Form a community group with your class. Make a trash sculpture. Collect plastic bottles, cans, foil wrappers, and other solid waste from your school cafeteria. Ask your principal for permission to put the sculpture outside. Choose a place where the public will see it. Make a large "RECYCLE" sign. Place it in front of the sculpture.

Draw a rough idea for a trash sculpture in the space below. Then compare your idea with those of your classmates. Use the best ones to make your sculpture.

Name _____  Date _____

*Critical Thinking*

All local governments must collect taxes. Taxes pay for schools, street repairs, police, fire, and other services. The county assessor decides how much tax people will pay on land, buildings, and other property they own. To do this, the assessor must figure out what the land and buildings are worth. This is called appraising.

**A. Using the information below, figure out the answers to the assessor's questions.**

Three lots in Joe Calvin's neighborhood sold this year. They sold for $60,000, $65,000, and $55,000. Figure out the average cost of a lot for question 1 below.

Three builders in the neighborhood charged $75, $85, and $80 a square foot to build homes. Figure out the average builder's cost in the neighborhood for question 2 below.

Mr. Calvin's new one-bedroom house is very small. It is twice the size of your classroom. Measure your classroom. Figure out the area in square feet for question 3 below.

Help the assessor appraise Joe Calvin's new house.

**1.** How much is Mr. Calvin's lot worth today, if its value is equal to the average cost of the three other lots?

_____

**2.** What have builders in Mr. Calvin's neighborhood charged for new houses this year?

_____

**3.** What is the size (in square feet) of Mr. Calvin's new house?

_____

**B. Contact your local county assessor's office. On the lines below, write three questions that you can ask the assessor or one of the assessor's aides.**

**1.** _____

_____

**2.** _____

_____

**3.** _____

_____

# 14 ▶ Comparing Letters to the Editor

**Exercise 48**

*Skill Practice*

Read the Letters to the Editor section in your local paper. People often use these letters to voice opinions about life in their city. Read the letters for several days. Choose four statements from different letters. Write the statements below on the first group of numbered lines. Then, on the next group of lines, write one or two sentences of your own telling whether you agree or disagree with the statement. Make sure you explain why you agree or disagree.

1. _____

_____

2. _____

_____

3. _____

_____

4. _____

_____

1. _____

_____

2. _____

_____

3. _____

_____

4. _____

_____

## 14 ▶ Identifying Fact and Opinion

**Exercise 49**

*Skill Practice*

Most letters to the editor contain the writer's opinions. However, some letters contain facts. Writers often use the facts to support their opinions.

**A.** Read the letter to the editor below. Then write *F* for fact or *O* for opinion on the lines after the sentences.

---

Editor:

   According to the U.S. Bureau of Labor Statistics, governments hire more people than private businesses. _____ This is a waste of taxpayer's money. _____ Our city hires twice as many workers as other cities of the same size. _____ So our city adds to the taxpayer waste. _____ Our city has the highest number of government workers in the state. _____ Before long, our local government will have no money for city services. People will go hungry. _____ Crime will rise. _____ Schools will fall apart. _____ The U.S. Bureau of Labor Statistics has more to say. It says that never in history have there been more workers in government than in private business. _____ Let's go back to the old way. _____ Let private business do the hiring. _____

Joan Tallmer

---

**B.** Now on the lines below, write your own letter to the editor. Use some facts to support your opinions. If you need more room, you can continue writing on a separate sheet of paper.

_____

_____

_____

_____

_____

_____

# 15 Role-Playing as a City Council Member    Exercise 50

*Critical Thinking*

**A.** You are a member of your local city council. What new laws do you want for your city? List five of them below.

1. _____

   _____

2. _____

   _____

3. _____

   _____

4. _____

   _____

5. _____

   _____

**B.** Your city does not have the money to establish all these new laws. Choose the two you feel most strongly about. On the lines below, explain the reasons for your choices.

_____

_____

_____

_____

_____

_____

_____

# 15 ▶ Interpreting Information

Sometimes, cities pass strange laws. At least, they seem to be strange on the surface. Cities make laws to solve certain problems—even if those problems are small ones.

Read the laws below. As recently as a few years ago, they were all real laws in American cities! After each law, write a problem that the law might have tried to solve. The first one is done for you.

Example:

**1.** It is illegal to put pennies in your ears in Honolulu, Hawaii.

*Possible problem:*

*Several children put pennies in their ears. One of them went deaf.*

**2.** It is illegal to push a baby carriage on the sidewalks in Logansport, Illinois.

*Possible problem:*

_____

_____

**3.** It is illegal to shoot open a can in Spades, Indiana.

*Possible problem:*

_____

_____

**4.** It is illegal to arrest a dead man for debts in New York City.

*Possible problem:*

_____

_____

**5.** Women jurors cannot knit in court in Mexico, Missouri.

*Possible problem:*

_____

_____

# 15 ▸ Becoming a Reporter

**Exercise 52**

*Critical Thinking*

One problem all communities have is graffiti (drawings or messages on public buildings). Most communities have local laws against graffiti. However, not everyone agrees graffiti is a bad thing. Some people feel that graffiti is another form of art.

**A.** Find out how your city feels about graffiti. What is your local law concerning graffiti? On the lines below, write the law in your own words.

_____

_____

_____

**B.** Now ask some people their opinions about graffiti. Interview your teachers, friends, family, and neighbors. Read them the law. What do they think about it? Is anyone in favor of graffiti in some cases? Does anyone feel your local law should be changed? Write the answers to your questions on the lines below.

**1.** _____

_____

**2.** _____

_____

**3.** _____

_____

**4.** _____

_____

**5.** _____

_____

**6.** _____

_____

Name _____ Date _____

**Exercise 53**

*Critical Thinking*

Each year, books are written about American cities and towns. These books rate the cities. The authors get facts about the cities, and then they use the facts to decide which cities offer the best services. The books rate the cities in the following areas:

1. Jobs
2. Crime
3. Health
4. Transportation

5. Education
6. The arts
7. Recreation
8. Environment

Now rate your city or town in the eight areas listed above. Give an *A* for excellent, a *B* for good, a *C* for fair, a *D* for poor, and an *F* for terrible. For any area that received a rating of *C* or poorer, write one or two sentences to suggest ways in which this area might be improved. Write your suggestions on the lines below.

Jobs
A   B   C   D   F

Education
A   B   C   D   F

Crime
A   B   C   D   F

The arts
A   B   C   D   F

Health
A   B   C   D   F

Recreation
A   B   C   D   F

Transportation
A   B   C   D   F

Environment
A   B   C   D   F

_____

_____

_____

_____

_____

_____

_____

_____

Name _____ Date _____

# 16 ► Filing a Claim in Small Claims Court                Exercise 54

You have created a design for a new machine you have invented. You have taken your design to a company, Patterson and Sons, to make your machine from your design. You give the company $5,000 as a down payment. The company promises to have your machine produced in four months. However, a year goes by, and it still is not completed. The company president insists the company will finish it soon, so he refuses to return your down payment. You are not satisfied with this situation. What can you do?

   You decide to take the company to Small Claims Court. Below is part of an actual Small Claims form. At the bottom, it says, "Briefly describe the nature of your claim." This means you should summarize what happened. Fill out the entire form. Add any other details you think would make your court case convincing. Use another sheet of paper if you need more room. Remember— your object is to *at least* get your $5,000 back!

---

PLAINTIFF'S STATEMENT

1. State your name and residence address, and the name and address of any other person joining with you in this action. If this claim arises from a business transaction, give the name and address of your business.

   a. Name _____

   Address _____ Phone No. _____
        Street

   _____
        City       State     Zip
   b. Name _____

   Address _____ Phone No. _____
        Street

   _____
        City       State     Zip

2. State the name and address of each person or business firm you are suing.
   If you are suing one or more individuals, give full name of each.
   If you are suing a business owned by an individual, give the name of the owner and the name of the business he/she owns.
   If your claim arises out of a vehicle accident, the driver and the registered owner of the other vehicle must be named.

   a. Name _____

   Address _____ Phone No. _____
        Street

   _____
        City       State     Zip
   b. Name _____

   Address _____ Phone No. _____
        Street

   _____
        City       State     Zip

3. State the amount you are claiming: $_____

Describe briefly the nature of your claim: _____

_____

_____

---

Name _____     Date _____

# 16 ▶ Interpreting Graphs

**Exercise 55**

*Skill Practice*

Crime rates in American cities rise or fall based on many factors, often economic ones. Local court systems are responsible for trying most criminal cases. Look at the bar graphs below. Then answer the questions on the following page.

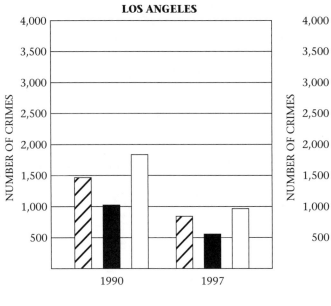

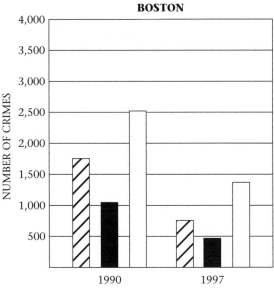

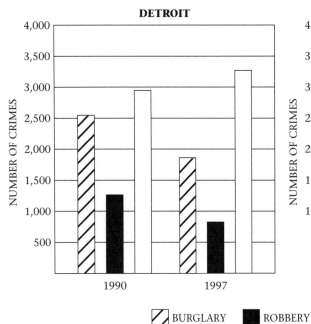

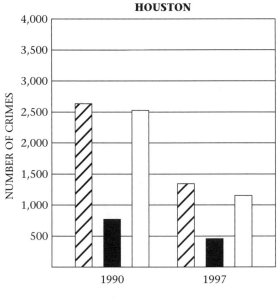

🖾 BURGLARY    ■ ROBBERY    ☐ AUTO THEFT

# 16 ▶ Interpreting Graphs (continued)

Exercise 55

*Skill Practice*

**Use the information from the graph to answer the questions below.**

1. In Los Angeles, which crime decreased the most between 1990 and 1997?

   _____

2. What was the difference in auto thefts in Los Angeles between 1990 and 1997?
   only a slight change               increased by about 50 percent
   decreased by about 50 percent     decreased by about 30 percent

3. What was the total number of robberies in Detroit in 1997?
   about 1,000          about 2,000          about 3,000          about 4,000

4. Did the number of auto thefts decrease in all the cities between 1990 and 1997? If not, in which city or cities did it increase?

   _____

5. Which city had the biggest decrease in burglaries between 1990 and 1997?

   _____

6. Which two cities had nearly the same number of auto thefts in 1997?

   _____

7. Which city reported the lowest number of any one crime in both 1990 and 1997? Which crime was it?

   _____

8. What was the total number of crimes reported by Boston in 1997?
   about 2,000          about 3,000          about 3,500          about 2,500

9. Which city had the largest number of crimes overall in 1990? In 1997?

   _____

10. Which city had the least number of crimes overall in 1990? In 1997?

   _____

# 17 ▸ Understanding a Supreme Court Decision    Exercise 56

*Critical Thinking*

In 1962, the U.S. Supreme Court heard a very important case. The case was called *Engel* v. *Vitale,* but it came to be known as "the school prayer case." This case came from New York State. The State Board of Regents there had asked public schools to adopt a prayer. The prayer was simple. It asked God to bless the children, their parents, the teachers, and the United States. Students were not forced to say the prayer. It was voluntary.

Ten families went to court claiming that even the voluntary prayer violated the First Amendment. The state courts disagreed. They ruled against the families. Finally, the case went all the way to the Supreme Court.

One justice, Potter Stewart, argued in favor of school prayer. He made these points:

---

1. The prayer is short and voluntary. How could such a short prayer hurt anyone's religious beliefs?

2. Religion is part of our nation's history. If children cannot pray in school, they cannot share fully in our nation's history.

3. Without school prayer, some children's freedom of religion is taken away.

4. Without school prayer, the schools seem to say that prayer is not important.

**Justice Hugo Black argued against school prayer. He made these points:**

1. The schools are part of the government. The prayer in New York is Christian. With this prayer, the government seems to favor the Christian religion.

2. School prayer violates the Constitution. The Constitution says the government cannot establish one religion over any other.

3. Early colonists came to America for religious freedom. In England, there was a national religion. This made true freedom of religion impossible. School prayer in America would hurt our country's tradition of freedom.

---

The other Supreme Court justices agreed with Justice Black. The Court voted 8–1 against school prayer. Still, many people today favor allowing voluntary school prayer. How do you feel about this issue? On a separate sheet of paper, write two or three sentences to answer the questions below.

1. You are a teacher. Five students want to pray quietly in class for a few minutes each morning. What will you tell them?

2. Your teacher decides to pray out loud each day. She writes a short prayer on the board and invites students to pray with her. The prayer is voluntary. What would you do?

3. Do you think school prayer violates religious freedom?

4. Does forbidding prayer in schools violate religious freedom?

# 17 Understanding State Laws on Religion     Exercise 57

**Read the article below. Then answer the questions that follow.**

In 1985, an Alabama law was brought before the U.S. Supreme Court. The laws allowed one minute of silence for prayer in public schools. The Supreme Court justices struck down the law. They said the First Amendment to the Constitution gives people freedom of religion. They decided that prayer in the public schools forces religion on students.

Since 1985, about one-half of the states in the United States have passed new laws. These laws allow students to have one minute of silence each day in the classroom. The laws says nothing about prayer. In New Jersey, one such law was struck down by a federal appeals court. It said the law was just another way of letting students pray.

Some members of the New Jersey legislature appealed the case to the U.S. Supreme Court. These representatives said that the moment of silence helped calm students down. If the students wanted to pray, it was up to them. In 1987, the Supreme Court decided not to review the case.

**1.** Which state passed a 1985 law allowing one minute of silence for school prayer?

_____

**2.** What happened when that state law was heard before the U.S. Supreme Court?

_____

**3.** On what grounds did the Supreme Court issue its ruling on the 1985 state law?

_____

**4.** What court ruled against the New Jersey state law?

_____

**5.** How was the New Jersey law different from the Alabama law?

_____

_____

**6.** What happened to the New Jersey law because the Supreme Court decided not to review the case?

_____

_____

# 17 ▶ Profiling a Religious Figure                        Exercise 58

*Skill Practice*

Each of the people listed below played an important role in establishing freedom of religion in the United States. Look up one of these people in an encyclopedia or on the Internet. Then write a brief essay profiling this person. Be sure to describe the person's contribution in the area of religious freedom.

| | |
|---|---|
| Roger Williams | William Penn |
| Anne Hutchinson | Joseph Smith |

_____

_____

_____

_____

_____

_____

_____

_____

_____

_____

_____

_____

_____

_____

_____

_____

_____

## 18 ▶ Creating a Political Cartoon                    Exercise 59

For more than a hundred years, political cartoons have appeared in our nation's newspapers and magazines. The artists who draw them have used them to criticize and often make fun of government — and the people who work in it. Political cartoons are a perfect example of the guarantee of freedom of the press that we enjoy in our country.

Thomas Nast was a political cartoonist during the 1800s. He is called the "father of political cartoons." Below is one of his cartoons from 1871. In this cartoon, Nast attacked the government in New York City. He felt the government was stealing people's money. His cartoons later helped force the dishonest men out of office.

"STOP THIEF!"

Draw your own political cartoon on a separate sheet of paper. It does not have to be about politics. For example, it can show something about your school or your neighborhood. However, your cartoon should have a "point of view," either to criticize, approve, or make fun of something. If you cannot draw a cartoon, clip out three or four good examples of political cartoons from some newspapers or magazines, and attach them to this sheet.

## 18 ▶ Understanding the McCarthy Period                    Exercise 60

**Read the passage below. Then answer the questions that follow.**

During the 1950s, freedom of speech in America was in trouble. The United States was in the middle of a "Cold War" with two communist countries: the Soviet Union and Red China. In the Soviet Union and China, there was only one political party: the Communist Party. In the United States, there were many political parties. One of them was the Communist Party.

During the 1940s and 1950s, the Communist Party in the United States had many members. It was not illegal to join the party. However, many congressmen in Washington, D.C. did not like this. They thought American Communists might help the Soviet Union, not their own country. They wanted American Communists fired from their jobs. The House of Representatives set up a committee to investigate members of the Communist Party. It was called the House Committee on Un-American Activities (HUAC).

The HUAC held hearings to look into communist influence on the film industry in 1947. People were called before this committee and asked, "Are you now or have you ever been a member of the Communist Party?" If they said yes, they were in trouble. If they refused to answer, they were in trouble. Many people would not answer any of the committee's questions. They claimed the 5th Amendment of the U.S. Constitution gave them the right to do this. The committee disagreed. A lot of people lost their jobs, and some even went to jail.

**1.** Which two countries were involved in a Cold War with the United States?

_____

**2.** Why were American Communists under attack during the 1950s?

_____

**3.** Who wanted American Communists fired from their jobs and put in jail?

_____

**4.** Do you agree or disagree that a person's right to free speech would be violated by having to answer the committee's questions? Explain why.

_____

_____

_____

# 18 ▶ Completing a Story

David Kwan works for a radio station in his country. One weekend, he visits a friend in a small town. Near this town is a nuclear power plant. David's friend says the plant leaks poison waste. People in the town are getting sick.

David looks into the problem. He takes some soil from the town to a scientist. The scientists tests the soil. The soil has poison waste in it! David goes to see the town doctors. They say many people in the town have become very ill, and some have developed cancer. David calls the people who run the power plant. No one there will give him a straight answer to his questions. That evening, David puts together a radio report on the town and the nuclear power plant.

**What do you think happened next? Choose one of the possibilities below, and write a paragraph or two to extend the story.**

**Story option 1:** David's radio report goes on the air. In this country, there is no guarantee of freedom of the press. The next day. . . .

_____

_____

_____

_____

_____

**Story option 2:** David's radio report goes on the air. The head of the nuclear power plant hears it. He calls David. He is very angry. This country guarantees freedom of the press. The next day. . . .

_____

_____

_____

_____

_____

# 18 ▶ Identifying Statements

Exercise 62

*Critical Thinking*

You read in your textbook that there are both protections and limits on freedom of speech and the press. Look at the statements below. Decide whether each one describes an act that is *protected* by the Constitution or one that has been *limited* by the Supreme Court. Write either *P* or *L* next to each statement.

_____ **1.** A man stands on a street corner and yells loudly that the mayor of his town is doing a lousy job.

_____ **2.** Two people stand up at the mayor's press conference and claim the mayor cheated them out of their life's savings. They know they have no evidence to back up their claim.

_____ **3.** A group of people put out a pamphlet that states the entire Supreme Court should be impeached because none of the justices knows anything about the Constitution.

_____ **4.** A newspaper prints a story that says the governor hired ten of her relatives for highly paid state jobs and none of them has ever shown up for work.

_____ **5.** A man in a basketball arena cannot find a seat. So he yells out, *Fire!* even though he knows there is not one.

_____ **6.** A state government tries to prevent a newspaper from publishing a story the government thinks may be embarrassing to the state.

_____ **7.** A newspaper wants to publish a story that reveals the location of all the country's nuclear missiles.

_____ **8.** An artist paints a picture that is not popular with everyone in her town. The city council votes to force the artist to destroy the painting.

_____ **9.** A magazine knowingly publishes a false story that says the mayor borrowed money from the city treasury and did not pay it back.

_____ **10.** Students at a high school wear small peace symbols on their lapels to protest the country sending troops to fight in another land. The principal has the students suspended from school.

# 18 ▶ Using a Code

**Exercise 63**

*Review*

By filling in the blanks below with the correct words from the following list, you will discover a code. Each number represents the letter above it. Using the code, find the answer to the question at the bottom of the page.

| | | | |
|---|---|---|---|
| information | obscene | express | protest |
| prior restraint | libel | slander | |

**1.** An order to prevent someone from doing something

‾‾ ‾‾ ‾‾ ‾‾ ‾‾   ‾‾ ‾‾ ‾‾ ‾‾ ‾‾ ‾‾ ‾‾ ‾‾
3  5  6  11  5   5  7  4  2  5  9  6  1  2

**2.** Facts; knowledge given or received

‾‾ ‾‾ ‾‾ ‾‾ ‾‾ ‾‾ ‾‾ ‾‾ ‾‾ ‾‾ ‾‾
6  1  10  11  5  12  9  2  6  11  1

**3.** To write or broadcast something untrue about someone to harm that person

‾‾ ‾‾ ‾‾ ‾‾ ‾‾
15  6  13  7  15

**4.** To say or show what you think or feel

‾‾ ‾‾ ‾‾ ‾‾ ‾‾ ‾‾ ‾‾
7  20  3  5  7  4  4

**5.** To make a statement against something

‾‾ ‾‾ ‾‾ ‾‾ ‾‾ ‾‾ ‾‾
3  5  11  2  7  4  2

**6.** Something that offends the public sense of decency

‾‾ ‾‾ ‾‾ ‾‾ ‾‾ ‾‾ ‾‾
11  13  4  17  7  1  7

**7.** To say something untrue about someone to harm that person

‾‾ ‾‾ ‾‾ ‾‾ ‾‾ ‾‾ ‾‾
4  15  9  1  19  7  5

**What do laws establish for freedom of speech and the press?**

‾‾ ‾‾ ‾‾ ‾‾ ‾‾ ‾‾ ‾‾ ‾‾ ‾‾ ‾‾ ‾‾   ‾‾ ‾‾ ‾‾   ‾‾ ‾‾ ‾‾ ‾‾ ‾‾ ‾‾
3  5  11  2  7  17  2  6  11  1  4   9  1  19   15  6  12  6  2  4

# 19 ▶ Understanding Point of View                    **Exercise 64**

---

An animal rights group has organized a protest at a lab. Inside the lab, scientists use live animals to test new drugs. The members of the group are against this. They say live animals do not need to be used in labs. The scientists disagree. They say animals are the best way to test new drugs before having people use them.

The protest goes on for weeks. The protesters carry signs and form a picket line. They try to get lab workers to go home. There is no violence. Then one day, a protester goes behind the lab to the parking lot. A scientist gets out of his car and walks toward the lab. The protester attacks the scientist. There is a fight. The scientist is injured and has to go to the hospital.

Now the government has a problem. Should it stop such protests at the lab? Are the lab workers' civil rights in danger? What about freedom of assembly for the animal rights group?

---

**A.** Take the point of view of the animal rights group. Write a brief essay that argues that the government should continue to allow the protests. Freedom of assembly should not be denied.

_____

_____

_____

_____

_____

**B.** Now take the opposite point of view. Write a brief essay that argues that the safety and civil rights of the lab workers are in danger. The government must halt the protests.

_____

_____

_____

_____

_____

# 19 ▶ Writing a Petition

You read in Chapter 19 of your textbook about the rights of groups to petition. You have read about petitions with legal power (initiatives, referendums, and recalls) as well as unofficial petitions. On the lines below, write a paragraph for an unofficial petition. The subject of your petition can be something of concern to your school, your neighborhood, or your entire town. Remember that the goal of a petition is to get as many signatures as possible so that your strong support will cause the government to take notice.

_____

_____

_____

_____

_____

_____

_____

_____

_____

_____

_____

_____

_____

# 19 ▶ Profiling a Historical Figure

**Exercise 66**

Each of the people listed below made strong use of the freedom to assemble and petition during his or her lifetime. Look up one of these people in an encyclopedia, other reference book, or on the Internet. Write a brief biographical profile. Detail how the subject used the freedom to assemble and freedom to petition to accomplish a change in government policy.

| | |
|---|---|
| Dr. Martin Luther King, Jr. | Susan B. Anthony |
| César Chávez | Carry Nation |

_____

_____

_____

_____

_____

_____

_____

_____

_____

_____

_____

_____

_____

_____

_____

_____

_____

**20 ▸ Designing a Poster or an Ad**                    **Exercise 67**

*Critical Thinking*

Design a poster or write a newspaper ad for a company or business you own.
The poster or ad should tell all about your business, including the kinds of
people you hire. Remember that it is against the law to discriminate when you
hire people. You can choose the type of company you run from those listed in
the box. Or you can make up one of your own.

| | |
|---|---|
| a clothing store | a fast-food restaurant |
| a video rental store | a company that makes airplane parts |
| a company that makes computers | |

# 20 ▶ Using a Code

By filling in the blanks below with the correct words from the following list, you will discover a code. Each number represents the letter above it. Using the code, find the answer to the question at the bottom of the page.

| equal protection | physical disability | due process |
|---|---|---|
| manager | discrimination | equal opportunity |

**1.** The act of treating unfairly

‾ ‾ ‾ ‾ ‾ ‾ ‾ ‾ ‾ ‾ ‾ ‾ ‾ ‾
8  3  7  2  6  3  1  3  9  4  5  3  10  9

**2.** Someone whose job is to oversee or supervise a group of workers

‾ ‾ ‾ ‾ ‾ ‾ ‾
1  4  9  4  11  14  6

**3.** To receive the same treatment under the law as everyone else

‾ ‾ ‾ ‾ ‾    ‾ ‾ ‾ ‾ ‾ ‾ ‾ ‾ ‾ ‾
14 12 16  4  13    17  6  10  5  14  2  5  3  10  9

**4.** The way laws are carried out to protect people's rights

‾ ‾ ‾    ‾ ‾ ‾ ‾ ‾ ‾ ‾
8  16  14    17  6  10  2  14  7  7

**5.** An injury to the body that keeps a person from moving the way able-bodied people do

‾ ‾ ‾ ‾ ‾ ‾ ‾ ‾    ‾ ‾ ‾ ‾ ‾ ‾ ‾ ‾ ‾ ‾
17 15 18  7  3  2  4  13    8  3  7  4  20  3  13  3  5  18

**6.** To receive the same chance as everyone else to do something

‾ ‾ ‾ ‾ ‾    ‾ ‾ ‾ ‾ ‾ ‾ ‾ ‾ ‾ ‾ ‾
14 12 16  4  13    10 17 17 10  6  5  16  9  3  5  18

**What failed to become law even though 35 states ratified it?**

‾ ‾ ‾ ‾ ‾    ‾ ‾ ‾ ‾ ‾ ‾
14 12 16  4  13    6  3  11  15  5  7

‾ ‾ ‾ ‾ ‾ ‾ ‾ ‾ ‾
4  1  14  9  8  1  14  9  5

# 20 ▶ Understanding the ERA

**Exercise 69**

*Critical Thinking*

> The people who supported the Equal Rights Amendment tried for ten years to get it passed. In 1982, they finally gave up. The ERA failed to become the Twenty-Seventh Amendment to the Constitution because only 35 of the required 38 states ratified it. Had the ERA become part of the Constitution, it would have granted equal rights to all women in all areas of American society. Do you think equal rights for women is a good idea? Why do you think many people were against the amendment—enough people in certain states to prevent it from becoming law?

**On the lines below, write a brief essay stating your position—either for or against the ERA. If you are in favor of it, discuss all the positive effects it would have had on American life if it had passed. If you are against it, describe what negative effects you think it would have had on American life if it had passed.**

_____

_____

_____

_____

_____

_____

_____

_____

_____

_____

_____

_____

# 20 ▶ Predicting What Might Have Happened    **Exercise 70**

---

In 1951, Linda Brown of Topeka, Kansas, was starting kindergarten. There was a grade school across the street from her house. However, Linda could not go there. Linda was black. The school was for whites only. Linda would have to walk two miles to the nearest all-black school. Linda's father, Oliver Brown, thought that his daughter was being discriminated against. He sued the city board of education.

A well-known African American lawyer took the case. His name was Thurgood Marshall. He took the Browns' case all the way to the U.S. Supreme Court. Marshall argued that the separate-but-equal law that allowed different schools for black and white students was unconstitutional. He said that African American children had separate schools. The schools were not equal. They were not as good as white schools. They were not given as much money as the white schools either. The Supreme Court agreed. In 1954, the Court unanimously ruled that segregation was unconstitutional.

At that time, the schools in some cities were not the only things that were segregated. Many parks, restaurants, and other public facilities around the country were also segregated. However, after the Brown decision, that began to end. The Supreme Court ruling helped start the Civil Rights Movement. In 1967, Thurgood Marshall became the first African American Supreme Court justice.

---

**What if the Supreme Court had ruled against Oliver Brown? What do you think might have happened? Write two or three sentences to answer the questions below.**

**1.** Would African American children today be getting as good an education as white children? Give reasons for your answer.

_____

_____

_____

**2.** Do you think there would be different schools around the country for Hispanics and other minorities? Why or why not?

_____

_____

_____

**3.** If the Court had ruled against the Browns, how different might our entire country be today? (Answer this question on a separate sheet of paper.)

Name _____  Date _____

You read in Chapter 20 that the government has certain laws about equal opportunity in three important areas: housing, education, and jobs. On the lines below, write three paragraphs summarizing the problems that once existed in each area and how government laws have solved these problems.

Housing

_____

_____

_____

_____

_____

_____

Education

_____

_____

_____

_____

_____

_____

Jobs

_____

_____

_____

_____

_____

_____

# 21 ▶ Identifying Legal and Illegal Actions

**Exercise 72**

*Critical Thinking*

**Read each statement below. Then decide whether it describes a legal action or an illegal action. Write either *L* or *I* on the line next to each statement.**

___ **1.** A police officer is writing up a parking ticket. When he finishes, he decides to search the trunk of the car for any illegal drugs.

___ **2.** A federal government agent has been following a suspicious-looking woman for two days. The woman checks into a hotel and later goes out for dinner. While she is out, the agent breaks into her hotel room to search it.

___ **3.** The police enter a home without a warrant to search it. They believe the evidence they are looking for is about to disappear.

___ **4.** The police arrive at a house with a search warrant. The owner of the house will not agree to the search, but the police force their way in and search anyway.

___ **5.** A police officer stops a driver for speeding. While she is writing up the ticket, she notices what appears to be illegal guns in the back seat. She tells the driver to get out of the car. Then she searches it.

___ **6.** A federal government agent suspects that a local businessman is conducting illegal activities from his office. While the businessman is out to lunch, the agent enters and searches the man's office.

___ **7.** A federal government agency believes a small group is plotting to smuggle illegal weapons into the country. The agency secretly plants a tape recorder in the local social club where the group meets once a week. The tape recorder is activated every time a conversation begins. After two weeks, the agency collects the tape recorder. The agency presents its evidence to a judge.

___ **8.** A federal agency presents evidence to a judge showing that a small group is plotting to kill a visiting foreign leader. The judge says the evidence is solid and grants a warrant. The agency then puts a tap on all the telephones inside the small group's headquarters to learn more details of the plot.

**21 Writing About the ACLU**

**Exercise 73**

*Critical Thinking*

The American Civil Liberties Union (ACLU) is a special interest group that works to protect the rights of all people. Over the years, the ACLU has taken some very controversial and unpopular cases.

**Look up the ACLU in an encyclopedia or other reference book or on the Internet. Read about the history of the group and the kinds of cases it has taken. Then, on the lines below, write a brief essay telling whether or not you think having an organization such as the ACLU is a good thing for our country. Also, tell whether you think organizations such as the ACLU exist in other countries, including nondemocratic ones.**

_____

_____

_____

_____

_____

_____

_____

_____

_____

_____

_____

_____

# 21 ▶ Categorizing News Articles

Read your newspaper for several days. Clip out as many articles as you can find that deal with the issue of privacy. These articles could involve court cases, arrests of suspects, or other matters that deal with privacy. Summarize the articles, and then decide whether each article describes an action that was legal or illegal under the Constitution's privacy laws. Write each summary in the correct category in the chart.

**Legal**

**Illegal**

Name _____ Date _____

# 22 ▶ Writing About Drug Testing

**Exercise 75**

*Critical Thinking*

One of today's most talked-about matters concerning privacy is drug testing. Over the past few years, the courts have ruled in many cases that involve testing people for drugs. Does the government have the right to test government employees for drugs? Does a private company have the right to ask a person looking for a job to take a drug test before being hired? Should people who have jobs where the safety of others is involved—such as airline pilots—be required to take drug tests? How about student athletes? Should high school and college athletes be asked to take drug tests before being allowed to join a team?

**Sometimes in a few cases, the courts have ruled that drug testing is legal. Often, the courts have ruled that drug testing is an invasion of privacy. What do you think? When, if ever, should drug testing be allowed? On the lines below, write an essay telling how you feel about the issue of drug testing.**

_____

_____

_____

_____

_____

_____

_____

_____

_____

_____

_____

_____

_____

_____

## 22 ▶ Sequencing the Order of Arrest

**Exercise 76**

**The sentences below describe the steps from the time a person is placed under arrest. The steps are out of order. Write the sentences in the correct order on the lines below. You may review Chapter 22 in your textbook if you need help.**

The suspect is warned that anything he or she says can be used in court.

The police read the suspect his or her rights.

The suspect can end the questioning at any time.

The police show the suspect an arrest warrant.

The police take the suspect's photo.

The suspect can call his or her lawyer.

The police take the suspect's fingerprints.

The police write up the arrest.

The police question the suspect.

The police arrest the suspect.

The suspect is informed that he or she has the right to remain silent.

The suspect is taken to the police station.

**Write your sentences here.**

1. _____
2. _____
3. _____
4. _____
5. _____
6. _____
7. _____
8. _____
9. _____
10. _____
11. _____
12. _____

Name _____  Date _____

## 22 Profiling a Historical Figure

### Exercise 77

Clarence Darrow was one of the most famous criminal lawyers in history. He took on many controversial cases to protect the rights of the accused. Darrow defended many suspects who were guilty, and he defended many innocent people, too. Some of Darrow's cases helped bring changes in our laws. These changes gave rights to future defendants. Darrow always fought for the rights of the accused.

**Look up Clarence Darrow in the encyclopedia or other reference or on the Internet. Then complete the profile below.**

### Profile of Clarence Darrow

Birth date: _____  Birthplace: _____

Home state: _____

School background: _____

_____

_____

Work background: _____

_____

_____

_____

Important cases: _____

_____

_____

_____

_____

## 22 ▸ Studying the Miranda Case

**Exercise 78**

*Review*

**Answer the questions below concerning the case of Ernesto Miranda.**

**1.** Who was Ernesto Miranda?

_____

**2.** Who arrested him?

_____

**3.** What crimes was he charged with?

_____

**4.** How did the police come to charge Miranda with the crimes?

_____

**5.** Why was Miranda found guilty in court?

_____

**6.** Who overturned Miranda's conviction?

_____

**7.** On what grounds was the conviction overturned?

_____

_____

**8.** What kind of lasting effect did Miranda's case have on the U.S. judicial system?

_____

_____

_____

_____

Name _____  Date _____

# 22 ▸ Explaining the Rights of the Accused          **Exercise 79**

**Read each case below. Then decide whether the statement that follows is True or False. Write *T* or *F* on the line before each case. Then, on the lines below, tell why the statement was either True or False.**

1. Catherine Willis is arrested for burglary. The police question her for several hours, and she confesses. Later, her lawyers find out that the police never gave her the Miranda warning.

   _____ The police cannot use any statements but can use other evidence.

   _____

   _____


2. Officer Melendez stops Bill Harris on the street and asks who he is.

   _____ Without arresting Bill, Officer Melendez can search him for anything illegal.

   _____

   _____


3. The police arrest Paul Emerson. On the way to the police station, the officers question him. Paul says some things that make him sound guilty. At the station, the police give the Miranda warning and question him again. He makes some more harmful statements.

   _____ As evidence, the police can use all the statements because Paul made them of his own free will.

   _____

   _____


4. Karen Davis has been arrested. A store clerk said she saw Karen shoplift something.

   _____ When the police ask Karen questions, she can stay silent until she gets a lawyer.

   _____

   _____

▶ 23 ▸ **Completing Cluster Maps**                                    **Exercise 80**

Look at the cluster maps below. In the outside circles, fill in the rights of
an accused person before trial, during trial, and after trial. You may review
Chapter 23 in your textbook if you need help.

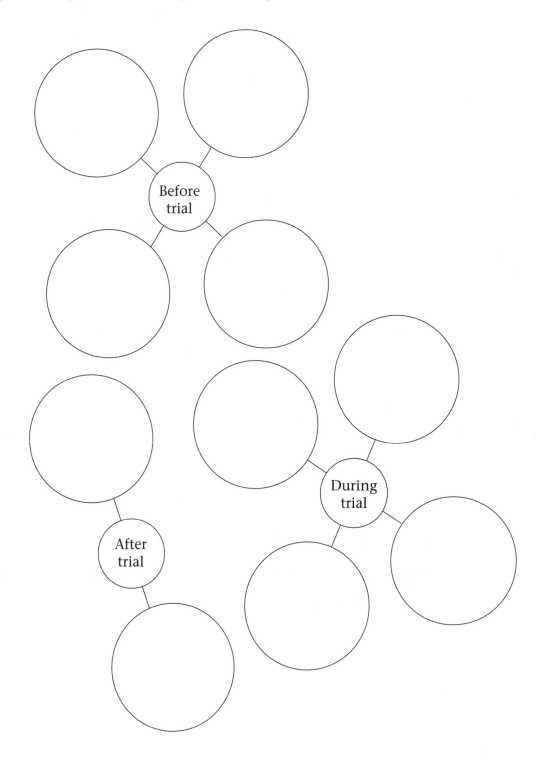

# 23 ▶ Matching Word Definitions

**Exercise 81**

*Review*

Match the words in Column A with the word or words that mean the same thing in Column B.

**Column A**

___ **1.** prosecute

___ **2.** defend

___ **3.** expert

___ **4.** impartial

___ **5.** verdict

___ **6.** venue

**Column B**

**a.** place

**b.** decision

**c.** present a case against

**d.** authority

**e.** present a case for

**f.** fair

Now use each of the words from Column A above in sentences of your own.

**1.** _____

_____

**2.** _____

_____

**3.** _____

_____

**4.** _____

_____

**5.** _____

_____

**6.** _____

_____

## 23 ▶ Picking a Jury

**Exercise 82**

*Critical Thinking*

Before a jury is selected for a trial, potential jurors are questioned by the judge, the defense lawyer, and the prosecutor. The judge asks the candidates questions to see if they will be good, fair jurists. The defense lawyer wants to be sure they will be fair to the defendant. The prosecutor wants people willing to convict the accused if there is enough evidence.

Pick a jury for the following case:

> A homeowner wakes up in the night. Someone is trying to break into her house. She takes a gun from under her pillow and shoots the intruder coming in the window. The intruder, who is seriously wounded, turns out to be a homeless person who was looking for shelter. He is unarmed. The homeowner is charged with aggravated assault for shooting an unarmed person.

On the lines below, write three questions the defense lawyer might ask a potential juror. Then write three questions the prosecutor might ask a potential juror.

1. _____

_____

2. _____

_____

3. _____

_____

4. _____

_____

5. _____

_____

6. _____

_____

Name_____  Date_____

# 24 ▶ Registering to Vote                          **Exercise 83**

**A.** Before being allowed to vote, citizens must fill out a voter registration form. These forms can be found in many places, including your local city hall, libraries, and many state motor vehicle bureaus. Below is a sample voter registration form. Fill it out.

| | |
|---|---|
| PRINT IN INK                                   For U.S. Citizens Only | |
| **1** Optional  ☐ Mr   ☐ Mrs   ☐ Miss   ☐ Ms<br>Name   (first)       (middle)        (last) | **11** PRIOR REGISTRATION<br>Have you ever been registered to vote?<br>Yes ☐   No ☐<br>If yes, complete this section to the best of your knowledge concerning your most recent registration. |
| **2** Residence      (No.      Street      Apt. No.) | |
| City          County          ZIP Code | Name (as registered) |
| **3** If no street address, describe location of residence: (cross streets, route, box, section, township, range, etc.) | Former Address |
| | City          County          State |
| | Political Party |
| **4** Mailing Address (if different) | **READ THE WARNING AND STATEMENT PRIOR TO SIGNING**<br>**I am a citizen of the United States** and will be at least 18 years of age at the time of the next election. I am not imprisoned or on parole for the conviction of a felony. I certify under **penalty of perjury** under the laws of the State of California, that the information on this affidavit is true and correct. |
| City          State          ZIP Code | |
| **5** Date of Birth<br>(mo      / day      / year      )  **8** Occupation | **WARNING**<br>Perjury is punishable by imprisonment in state prison for two, three, or four years. § 126 Penal Code. |
| **6** Birthplace | |
| **7** Political Party (check one)<br>☐ American Independent Party<br>☐ Democratic Party<br>☐ Libertarian Party<br>☐ Reform Party<br>☐ Republican Party<br>☐ Decline to State<br>☐ Other_____ (Specify) | **9** Telephone (Optional)<br>Area Code (   )<br><br>**10** I prefer election materials in:<br>(Check one)<br>☐ English  ☐ Spanish<br>OFFICE USE | **12** Signature<br>▶<br><br>Date<br>▶<br><br>**13** Signature of person assisting (if any) |

**B.** Now on another sheet of paper, write a brief essay explaining why having the right to vote is such an important right in a democratic society.

## 24 ▶ Writing About Third Party Candidates

**Exercise 84**

*Skill Practice*

> For more than one hundred years, the two major American political parties have been the Democrats and Republicans. Every President since 1852 has been a representative from one or the other party. However, over the years, there have been third party candidates who, while they did not become President, gained much support in a particular presidential campaign.

Look at the names of the people listed in the box. Each one ran a third party campaign for President at one time during the 20th century. Look up one of the names in an encyclopedia or other reference or on the Internet. Then write a brief profile of the person. Be sure to include information about why the person ran for President, the name of the third party, the party's platform, and other issues that came up during this campaign.

| | | |
|---|---|---|
| Theodore Roosevelt | George Wallace | H. Ross Perot |
| Robert M. LaFollette | John Anderson | |

_____

_____

_____

_____

_____

_____

_____

_____

_____

_____

_____

## 24 ▸ Developing a Third Party                          **Exercise 85**

As you have already learned, there are two main political parties in the United States: the Republican Party and the Democratic Party.

In general, here are three things the Republican Party believes in:

1. private interests over government interests
2. more power to state government and less to the federal government
3. spend large amount of money on the military to guarantee a strong national defense

In general, here are three things the Democratic Party believes in:

1. government rules and regulations for private business
2. government provides many social services for citizens
3. a powerful federal government

The symbol for the Republican Party is the elephant. The symbol for the Democratic Party is a donkey.

**You want to start your own third party. What would it be called? What would it stand for? On the lines below, give your party a name, and write at least three things your party believes in or stands for. Then draw a symbol for your party at the bottom of this page.**

_____

_____

_____

_____

_____

Name _____  Date _____

**Explaining Political Terms**                          **Exercise 86**

*Review*

Look at each of the words in the list below. Explain in two or three sentences
what role each one plays in the political process of our country.

| political parties | national conventions | primary elections |
|---|---|---|
| delegates | party platforms | |

political parties _____

_____

_____

national conventions _____

_____

_____

primary elections _____

_____

_____

delegates _____

_____

_____

party platforms _____

_____

_____

88    Chapter 24 • Political Parties and the Right to Vote

Copyright © by Globe Fearon, Inc. All rights reserved.

Name _____     Date _____

# 24 ▷ Completing a Chart                                 **Exercise 87**

> The two major political parties in the United States are very active in local politics as well as national politics. Chances are that your local mayor, city council representative, state representative, or state senator is a member of either the Democratic or Republican party.

Contact at least three of your local representatives. Have their offices send you information about these officeholders. Ask for information such as party membership, a list of issues that are important to them, which bills they have sponsored (or what executive actions they have undertaken), and any other material that can help you learn about their work representing you and your neighbors. Then, on the chart below, list the name of the officeholder, and summarize this information in either the Democratic or Republican column.

| **Democrats** | **Republicans** |
|---|---|
| Name: _____ | Name: _____ |
| Issues: _____ | Issues: _____ |
| _____ | _____ |
| _____ | _____ |
| _____ | _____ |
| Name: _____ | Name: _____ |
| Issues: _____ | Issues: _____ |
| _____ | _____ |
| _____ | _____ |
| _____ | _____ |
| Name: _____ | Name: _____ |
| Issues: _____ | Issues: _____ |
| _____ | _____ |
| _____ | _____ |

## 25 ▸ Writing About National Service

**Exercise 88**

*Critical Thinking*

> All young men 18 to 25 years old are required to register with the Selective
> Service System. That means that they are eligible to be called up for military
> service in event of war. Many people today still feel that young, healthy American
> males—and some say females—should be required to serve their country in some
> way. These people say that even if we do not require military service, there should
> be some other form of required national service. This service could involve such
> things as working in cities to help the poor, helping underprivileged youngsters in
> bad neighborhoods, or performing some other community service as a way of
> fulfilling their responsibilities as citizens.

**What do you think? Should the government establish some form of required
national service? On the lines below, write an essay stating your views on
this issue.**

_____

_____

_____

_____

_____

_____

_____

_____

_____

_____

_____

# 25 ▸ Conducting a Census

**Exercise 89**

*Skill Practice*

In Chapter 25, you read about the census. You know that every ten years the federal government conducts a census of the entire population. The questions on this page are very similar to the ones the government asks in its census.

Use the questions to conduct a census of the households on your street. Choose a partner. Have an adult accompany you and your partner. Try to visit at least five different houses or apartments and get as much information as you can. *Do not force anyone to answer questions they do not want to.* Tell your neighbors you are doing this for a school project. If they still refuse to answer, thank them politely and go on to the next house. When you are done with the census, write up your results on a separate sheet of paper and bring it to class. Ask the teacher to hold a discussion about the class's findings or to post all the results on the bulletin board.

1. How many people live in your household?

2. How many adult men live in your household? What are their ages?

3. How many adult women live in your household? What are their ages?

4. How many male children under the age of 18 live in your household? What are their ages?

5. How many female children under the age of 18 live in your household? What are their ages?

6. What is the religion of your family?

7. What is the nationality of your family?

8. What are the occupations of the adults living in your household?

9. Do any of the children under the age of 18 have occupations? What are these occupations?

10. Does your family live in a single housing unit (house) or a multiple-family dwelling (apartment building)?

# 25 ▶ Charting the Federal Budget

## Exercise 90

*Critical Thinking*

One of the responsibilities of Americans is to pay taxes. People pay taxes to the federal government based on their income. In return, their tax money is used by the government to pay for services to the people. However, while Americans have to pay taxes, they do not really have a say in how their money is spent. Of course, at election time, the people have a right to vote out of office any politicians who decide to spend the taxpayers' money in ways the voters do not like. Until that time, though, Congress and the President plan a budget based on what they feel is necessary for the government to run effectively.

Look at the numbers in the chart below. They show government spending for several executive branch departments for the fiscal year 1999. How do you think the government has been spending the American taxpayers' money? Is too much money going for some things and not enough for others? Study the chart. Then, on a separate sheet of paper, make your own chart listing these same departments. Tell whether you would increase or decrease the budget for each department and why. If you wish to decrease spending in some area, tell what programs or things you would do away with. If you wish to increase spending, tell what things you would spend the additional money on.

| Executive Departments/Spending Fiscal 1999* | |
| --- | --- |
| **Department** | **Amount** |
| Agriculture | 62,885,000 |
| Commerce | 5,036,000 |
| Defense | 214,747,000 |
| Education | 33,521,000 |
| Energy | 16,079,000 |
| Health & Human Services | 359,700,000 |
| Housing & Urban Development | 32,736,000 |
| Interior | 7,773,000 |
| Justice (includes FBI, DEA, INS only) | 8,018,000 |
| Labor | 32,459,000 |
| State | 6,464,000 |
| Transportation | 41,819,000 |
| Treasury | 387,280,000 |
| Veterans' Affairs | 43,169,000 |
| *figures in millions of US dollars | |

**Source:** *The World Almanac* and *Book of Facts 2000*